eBay Selling Secrets Massive Profits

40 Secrets To Make Huge Money Buying At Thrift Stores And Reselling On eBay

Table of Contents

Introduction

Chapter 1: Finding Your Goods

Chapter 2: What Items Are Best to Resell on eBay?

Chapter 3: Listing Your Items to Sell on eBay

Chapter 4: Making Your Items Stand Out

Chapter 5: How Does eBay Work?

Chapter 6: Amazing Your Buyer

Chapter 7: Shipping Your Items for Top Customer Reviews

Conclusion

Introduction

I want to thank you and congratulate you for downloading the book, *eBay Selling Secrets for Massive Profits: 40 Secrets to Make Huge Money Buying at Thrift Stores and Reselling On eBay.*

This book contains proven steps and strategies on how to find items in your local thrift stores in order to sell for profits on eBay. eBay is the largest auction site on the internet for individuals to buy and sell items. Even though you may not realize it, a lot of these items were found in a thrift store and resold. Thrift stores are a prime source of goods that can be sold at a profit. Some of the most profitable thrift store items are bric a brac, electronics and books. In this book, I'm going to cover how to find such items and relist them to make a massive profit using eBay.

I'm sure that you have never seen items in a thrift store as a possible source of cash. Or have you? Even though thrift store items may be viewed as "give aways," people actually donate valuable and useable items without knowing it. By knowing how to scan the shelves and find what sells, you can turn around and sell your finds on eBay for a lot of extra cash! All you need is a little time, a thrift store, and an eBay seller account. This book will walk you through the entire process of finding sellable items to the eBay listing process. So, if you're ready to find a little extra cash, let's take a look at selling on eBay!

Thanks again for downloading this book, I hope you enjoy it!

© **Copyright 2015 by** _____Rick Riley_____ -
All rights reserved.

This document is geared towards providing exact and reliable information in regards to the topic and issue covered. The publication is sold with the idea that the publisher is not required to render accounting, officially permitted, or otherwise, qualified services. If advice is necessary, legal or professional, a practiced individual in the profession should be ordered.

- From a Declaration of Principles which was accepted and approved equally by a Committee of the American Bar Association and a Committee of Publishers and Associations.

In no way is it legal to reproduce, duplicate, or transmit any part of this document in either electronic means or in printed format. Recording of this publication is strictly prohibited and any storage of this document is not allowed unless with written permission from the publisher. All rights reserved.

The information provided herein is stated to be truthful and consistent, in that any liability, in terms of inattention or otherwise, by any usage or abuse of any policies, processes, or directions contained within is the solitary and utter responsibility of the recipient reader. Under no circumstances will any legal responsibility or blame be held against the publisher for any reparation, damages, or monetary loss due to the information herein, either directly or indirectly.

Respective authors own all copyrights not held by the publisher.

The information herein is offered for informational purposes solely, and is universal as so. The presentation of the information is without contract or any type of guarantee assurance.

The trademarks that are used are without any consent, and the publication of the trademark is without permission or backing by the trademark owner. All trademarks and brands within this book are for clarifying purposes only and are the owned by the owners themselves, not affiliated with this document.

Chapter 1- Finding Your Goods

Have you ever thought that you could make extra money from your local thrift store? Thrift stores are a breeding ground for people's unwanted goods. The great part about unwanted items is that people really don't stop and think about whether or not they're giving away a treasure or not. When going through your old items, do you look for items of value before you pack them up into boxes and send them for donation? I had never thought about this concept until I came across the idea of selling thrift store items on eBay. After reading about people making serious money from thrift store goods, I thought that it would be a good activity to take on. However, I was still a little lost on what I could sell on eBay.

Before you can consider selling items on an eBay account, you really must have items that can be sold. Your local thrift store is a mountain of possibilities. Thrift stores have an ever-changing inventory, so it makes it easier to go to one place and find new items. You can never know what to expect to find when you enter the doors. Taking a look at finding your items in a thrift store, I'm going to give you some great tips on how to find and get the best deals on thrift store items. Don't worry, it's not that hard and you will actually enjoy your thrift store shopping.

Choosing a thrift store

All thrift stores might seem to be the same to you. However, the inventory at thrift stores can vary by the thrift store's location. Depending on the items you're looking for, certain thrift stores might offer a better chance for you to find what you want. The population and its demographics around a thrift store can vastly influence the store's inventory and the types of items that are donated. For example, if you're looking for more valuable bric a brac, you might want to consider looking in a thrift store that is located in a wealthier part of town. The items here will be of higher quality and might earn you more when reselling.

Once you know what types of items you are looking for, find a thrift store that is more likely to carry that type of item. Frequent this thrift store on days when you know that new items are being put out. By going into the store and looking frequently, you will find the valuable items before others do.

Taking time to look

If you're on a time crunch then thrift store shopping isn't going to do you a lot of good. Since thrift stores take so many diverse items on a daily basis, you really need to have a good chunk of time to be able to really look over everything that the store offers. Another thing about thrift stores is that the same thrift store will never have the same inventory twice. Even though you frequent the same store, its offerings are constantly changing.

When going into your thrift store or stores, make sure that you have the time to really look at the shelves and items displayed.

If you're rushed or unable to take your time, you might overlook a great find. When looking through the items, observe their condition and possible value. If you have a smart phone, take a look at what similar items are selling for on eBay. Sometimes, the cost of the item is more than how much it will sell for. By taking your time and really going through your store, you can find items that will get you the most money.

Look for coupons and sales

If you frequent certain thrift stores, then you will more than likely know when they will be offering sales. Also, to make sure they get your repeat business, they will often give you coupons and advertisements for your next visit. Pay close attention to these ads because it could help you get your item at a great bargain, which will increase your profit when sold on eBay. Remember, you're trying to make extra money, so the less you spend in the thrift store and the more you sell it for, the more money you will make in the end. Be a bargain shopper even if it feels a little extreme!

Know when to shop

When visiting your thrift store, know which days are less shopped and have the better deals for the items you're looking for. If you're going to be rubbing elbows the whole time you're there, you won't be as inclined to take your time and really look. As you shop more and more, you will find that you will get a feel for when are the right times to shop and get the most out of your experience.

Try to have an inside contact

If at all possible, get to know some of the employees who work in the thrift stores that you frequent. By getting to know some people within the business, you can have an advantage of knowing when items come into the store early on. When items that interest you come up, then have them contact you and let you know. If they know the items that you purchase on a regular basis, then it will be to your advantage to know when would be a good time to go to that specific store.

Take a look at what's popular on eBay

Go onto the website and enter words such as "vintage" and "collectable" into the search bar. Take a look at the various listings in the different departments to determine what is selling and what is not so popular. Once you get a good idea of what is popular on the site, try looking for similar or the same items when going through your thrift store. Take your smart phone with you when you shop so that you can easily look up items that have caught your interest to see if they are a worthwhile investment. Use your resources to help you find what you can sell.

Once you know your local thrift shops and their common offerings, you will be able to better gauge what you would like to look for and why. In the next chapter, I'm going to cover what types of items tend to sell the best on eBay that can be found in your local thrift store. After getting a good idea of what sells and what to look for, then you will be ready to hit up all of your favorite shops and find items that will help you make a profit on eBay!

Chapter 2- What Items are Best to Resell on eBay?

Due to the setup of the eBay website, there are some types of items that will sell on the site better than others. Even though you will see it all when looking through the listings, some items simply do not sell and are not worth the time to buy and list. Knowing what you're looking for when doing your thrift store shopping will help you to save time and energy when shopping in a thrift store.

If you're not a frequent eBay shopper, you might not know what is getting the big bucks on it. Don't fear! We are going to explore eBay and the items you can find in your thrift store that will sell for a lot of cash. Not everything you see in a thrift store can be sold through eBay. Remember that it is an auction site and some items do not sell well within this type of format. In this chapter, I'm going to talk about some of the items you want to consider looking for to resell on eBay that will earn top dollar. However, you might find other odd items that you can sell as well!

Electronics

Even though you might think that electronics in a thrift store might be dysfunctional and not worth the money, the truth is that some of the electronics donated can be sold for a lot of money. For example, a lot of people are looking for electronic items such as classic Sony Walkmans and other older tech items that you would initially view as having little to no value. People are constantly looking for older electronics, so just because it means little to you, it might have great value to another.

My husband and I are avid eBay sellers and find that many of the electronics that we purchased from a local thrift store were sold for twice to three times as much as we purchased them for! It was a matter of finding working electronics that we knew were rare and listing them and selling them. So, a two dollar Walkman has just become a six dollar item. That's a four dollar profit. Of course, this is just an example, so the figures are not necessarily accurate!

When going through the electronics section, look for items that were popular when you were a child. Old gaming systems, stereos, and other various electronics might just be a hot item for you to sell on eBay. The great part about most thrift stores is that they provide an area to test out the item before purchase, so you can feel better about the condition of your purchase before you leave the store!

Books

Books are another item that can be sold on eBay. However, you want to find books that are either collectables, antiques, or rare. If it's a book that can be found almost anywhere, then the buyers will pass it by. When they look for books on eBay, they are looking for books with special characteristics, such as first editions, autographed copies, or rare books. For example, the Little Golden Books have a first edition that are worth a lot of money if found in a good condition. Be aware of books and how to find the ones that can be sold in an auction setting.

Toys

Many toys that can be found in a thrift store are collectable and will sell for good money on eBay. Older toys, such as collectible board games and Barbie dolls might be worth money if they are old enough and in demand. However, collectors won't want to buy these items unless they are in good or superior shape. So, before you purchase such toys, make sure that they are in decent shape or that you are able to clean them up.

Classic stuffed animals are also worth money. Get a feel for what an older toy or stuffed animal looks like and go in search of them in the toy section. Sometimes since children play with the toys, you might have to dig to find what might be a great find. So, be patient and see the possibilities in what you're looking at.

Figurines and glassware

Another great item to sell on eBay are figurines. If you walk into any thrift store, you will notice that there are aisles of figurines and home décor. Take a look through the clutter on these shelves to see if you can find items worth selling. Valuable figurines will have numbers on them that will place them as part of a limited collection. The lower the number, the better chance that it will be worth money. Also look to see if you can find rarer forms of popular collectables such as Precious Moments will be worth money.

Glassware that is older and more unique can have a significant value as well. These pieces are often mixed in with the other home décor and figurines or you might find them in the kitchen supplies. The key to finding items that worth money is to be patient and be willing to work through what might seem like mountains of junk.

Pens and writing accessories

It might sound silly, but people actually donate pens and writing accessories that can be worth some serious money. Thrift stores pack these in large bags and mix them with other office supplies. Many people don't know that there is value in some pens or pencils. However, pens and pencils made out of sterling silver and other metals or resin can snag some good money on eBay.

The secret to finding these is to know what types of pens are worth money and be willing to spend some time looking through all of the random grab bags to see if there is anything in them that is of worth.

Take some time and look at eBay's full website to get an idea of what you could sell that you have seen in your thrift store.

Once you see what sells, you will have an easier time finding what you're searching for when entering the doors. Knowing what to look for and where to find it are essential when finding thrift store items.

Where do we begin? If you're like most people, the thought of looking through the multiple racks of clothing might seem intimidating. I must admit that the first time I walked into a thrift store to look at clothing, I was completely overwhelmed. The whole store seemed to be covered with racks of clothing, and I was totally lost with the sheer volume of what lay before me. Where would I start and how in the world was I going to find what I was looking for? Since that moment in time, I have vowed that I would help others in the same situation.

By knowing what to look for, you will feel less intimidated by the sheer volume of clothing that thrift stores carry. Pick a place to start and begin to look for the characteristics outlined in this chapter to help you find what you're looking for.

Most people know what brands are the most luxurious and are really worth money. Ten to one is that you won't find any of these screaming out at you from the hanger. Even though you don't recognize the name on the label doesn't make it less valuable. So, what do you look for when looking through the racks of clothing?

Materials

Most clothing tends to be made of cotton or polyester, so when you see clothing that is made out of other types of fabrics, take a closer look at the item. Fact is that fabrics such as silk or leather are worth more to begin with than cotton. A silk blouse or leather jacket can easily be resold at a profit. However, when looking at these items, you really need to look at the listing of materials on the label. The more of the rarer material is present, the more likely that the piece will be worth more when resold. Take a closer look at the clothing that have the rarer materials and see if they are of enough quality for resale.

Condition of the Garment

Even if you find a piece of clothing that you believe could be worth some money when resold, then you really need to look at the full piece. If there is damage to the material, it isn't going to be worth as much as a piece of clothing that is in near flawless condition. When people buy clothing, they want it to be of near new quality, not torn, stained, or stretched. Take some time and really inspect the garment. Odds are that if you wouldn't buy it due to its condition, others will be less likely to as well.

The Label

Believe it or not, the label on a piece of clothing can tell you a lot about it. If you look at simple, every day clothing, you might notice that the tags are rather plan and all look alike. A good way to tell a quality piece of clothing is by looking at the tag. Look for the brand, the coloring of the tag and the details provided on the tag. The more elaborate the tag is, the higher quality the item. You will be looking at the tag for other selling elements, but the first impression is often a good clue as well.

Brand Names

Even though the top brands may not be starting back at you from the racks, brands do tend to carry a great detail about quality. While you might not find Prada and Gucci, you might be able to find some other top brands that can be sold at a great profit. Which brands do you look for?

Well, if you are looking for womens clothing to resell, you always want to keep an eye out for Eileen Fisher, St. John and Citron Santa Monica. These brands are stylish and have great resale value. Fendi, Guess, and Yves St Laurent are also top brands that can fetch a pretty penny when resold on eBay. If you're in doubt, take out your handy smart phone and take a look at the brand and its popularity!

You always want to be on the lookout for mens hawaiian shirts. You should be looking for brands like Tommy Bahama,

Jams World and Nat Nast among others. You always want to be looking for loud, vibrant designs when it comes to hawaiian shirts. Also, if you can find hawaiian shirt brands like Kahala and Tori Richard, they sell as well. However, you want to be purchasing those lower end hawaiian shirts at around the $2 range. Always remember, in general, the bigger the better! Do not pass up those XXL and XXXL size shirts thinking that no one is looking for those sizes. They will still sell and usually these big sizes will snatch a higher dollar value than the smaller ones! If you find a hawaiian shirt that catches your eye, make sure and do some research before making a decision. There are many vintage hawaiian shirts that you may come across that could be worth big money. However, they may take a quick bit of research to see if it sells. You don't want to leave a $100 vintage shirt behind because you were unsure if it sells!

Another thing you want to be looking for is athletic clothing. However, you are only going to be looking to buy this if it is still in good condition. Look for womens athletic brands such as Lululemon and Athleta. You can also sell Nike Fit Dry clothing for a good price on eBay, however, you are going to want to buy Nike in the $2-3 range. Look for cycling jerseys as well. These are tight fitting athletic looking jerseys. Usually they have 3 panel pockets on the back. Look for brands like Bianchi, Shimano and Primal Wear.

Always look for vintage mens skateboard and surf clothing. The vintage 1980's skateboard brands Vision Street Wear and Powell Peralta vintage clothing can fetch a pretty penny. These usually have very loud and vibrant designs. When it comes to vintage surfing brands, always pick up Lightning Bolt and vintage OP clothing.

Remember that every single thrift store that sells clothing has numerous profitable items inside. It is true that in this day and age many of the thrift stores are becoming more aware of the value of clothing items. It can be very frustrating seeing the price on some of the clothing items at the thrift store. However, they will always be overlooking some brands. The people pricing the clothing at the thrift store don't know everything. This is where you can take advantage and make some big time money! The more knowledge you acquire when it comes to what styles and brands sell, the more money you will be able to make every single time you step into the thrift store!

If you find a nice, high end clothing brand with a light blemish, do not move past it right away. Take a look at it and evaluate how bad the blemish is and if it is worth buying to sell as a long tail item. I can't tell you how many times I have bought a shirt with a tiny blemish and resold it for good money. However, when selling these items, remember to always describe and take clear pictures of the blemish. This will save you a lot of headaches when your customer receives the shirt.

Where the Clothing was Made

We all know that most of our clothes are made in the USA, Mexico or China. The cost to make and manufacture these clothes is less, making it possible for clothing companies to produce more product and make a better profit. However, have you seen clothes on the racks that are made in other countries? Look at your label closely. Garments made in European countries tend to be of higher quality and will sell for more. When you come across these items, take a closer look at them and research the brand on your smart phone. You might just have a great find in your hands!

Details on the Clothing

If you have a gut feeling that an item of clothing might be more valuable, don't be afraid to pull it off the rack and take a closer look at it. Some pieces tend to go unnoticed by the uninformed consumer. However, when looking at the piece of clothing, look at the details. Does the item have fancy buttons, embellishments, or any other marker that would signal to you that some time was taken in the production of it? Just because it might not sport a designer label doesn't meant that it isn't valuable.

Sizes

The harder to find sizes on a normal store's shelf are a great find when looking for items to resell. Top brands tend to make clothing for popular sizes because they sell better than items for people who are not typical sized. This includes plus sizes, extra-long pants, and other factors that are not considered typical. These items often sell for much more online than items that are made for the average person.

Vintage Items

The older and rarer the items are, the greater the likelihood that these items are going to sell better. Look for items of clothing that would have been worn in different decades. People are constantly looking for vintage items, so your find will more than likely bring a good resale price.

Let's summarize all of the information that we just took in here. When going to a garage sale or a thrift store, you want to take the time to really look at the items. The first thing you should examine is the material that the item is made from. If you feel that the piece is of finer quality, take a closer look at the tag. What is the content of materials in the piece? Where was the item manufactured? Does the tag look high quality? If you find that the item could be of value, take an even closer look at it. Is the material in good shape? Are there stains or tears? Would you buy it for your own use due to its condition?

Once you have taken a thorough look at all the characteristics of the garment in front of you, you will more than likely have a good idea of whether or not this piece can be resold for a profit. Knowing what to look for is the key to finding a great item to resell. Don't be afraid to take your time, look at the brand on your smartphone, and really examine your find before deciding to make your purchase!

Chapter 3- Listing Your Items to Sell on eBay

If you have never used eBay to sell in the past, the thought of selling items online might seem a little daunting to you. A lot of boundaries exist between people and their selling potential based on the fact that they don't feel comfortable with the online sales. However, a lot of business now comes from online sales, so don't miss out on the opportunity to make money simply because you feel intimidated by the website. In this chapter, I'm going to walk you through the methods of being able to maximize your profits by how you list your items on eBay.

Once you have items that are sellable on eBay, you need to know how to use the website to make sure you're getting the most out of the experience. As mentioned before, you must have a seller account in order to sell. This is easy to sign up for. eBay does charge you fees for items that you list and sell, so be aware of this when pricing your items. The site also asks you to set up a method in which you prefer to be paid by your buyers. I prefer to use PayPal as it is secure and easy to use.

Before you even think about listing your items, there are a few things you want to make sure you do so that you get the maximum value out of what you're selling. First of all, you want to have a detailed description of the item. This will include any damage that the item has, size, weight, and any other attribute that will give the buyer a clear picture of what to expect out of the item. Second of all, you want to have a good picture of the item. If the item has many sides, you will want to take pictures of all of them to ensure that the buyer gets to see all of the item. Last of all, you want to make sure that you start the item for bidding at a reasonable price that is below market value. People will bid on the item and bring the price up, so they won't be so inclined to bid if the item is priced high to begin with.

If you have an item that you know will sell at a set price, don't be afraid to use the option to sell it for a set price. People look for specific items all the time, and if you have what they're looking for, then they will want to buy it outright. The auction setting also gives you the option to sell it as a "buy it now." If the person wants the item badly enough, then they can skip the bidding and just buy the item for the amount that you request. Since there are different ways of selling your item, you have a better chance at getting what you want for the item that you have listed.

Once you have a suitable listing, you will want to set it up on the website and put in your choices of how long the auction goes, whether or not you will let the buyer buy it outright, and what method of payment you would prefer. The seller website walks you through these steps thoroughly, making it possible to cover everything that is needed in order to have a successful sale.

Think of what you would like to see a listing look like. What would you want to look at further? Try to duplicate these factors when designing your listing for the public. You want it to be thorough yet grasp the attention of those who are browsing the website. The more views you get, the better chance you will be able to sell your item for the price that you want it to sell for.

The next step is to actually open up the auction for bidding. If you have a longer running listing, you will want to check your messages daily to make sure you can answer questions that potential buyers may have. Good communication is good way to get positive feedback once the item sells. It might also increase the chances that you will get a better bid on the item.

If you're in doubt on how to list an item, take a look at similar items to what you're selling and get some ideas of how people describe and list them. By listing your item correctly and making it look good to the buyer, you will have a better chance at getting top dollar for your item. The more money the item makes, the more profit you will have!

Chapter 4- Making Your Items Stand Out

You're a savvy shopper, right? If you know what you're looking for, then finding it is easier if you find the items in a timely fashion. When online shopping, the products and items listed tend to have more activity if the listing stands out in some way. Since your goal is to make money using eBay, then it's a good idea to take a look at how to make a listing stand out to the scrolling buyer. In this chapter, I'm going to give you some tips on making any item stand out in the long list of offerings that flood eBay on a typical day.

If you ever scroll through the listings on eBay, what listings stand out to you and make you want to take a closer look at them? When selling your items, you really want to make sure that your listing gets as many views as possible. Making your listing stand out is a great way to make sure that you're getting as much money from the item as possible. Let's take a look at listings that you might want to click on so that you will able to do a similar listing for your own item.

Good picture

When listing your item, you want to make sure that the picture of the item is great and will give a true representation of what the item is. In order to do this, the camera needs to be able to pick up the details of the object. Try placing the item on a solid background that will complement the item and not drown it out. For items that are light in color, a darker background will help it to stand out. Darker items will stand out better on lighter backgrounds. When taking the picture, make sure that the lighting in the area is good and that the item is positioned so that it photographs well. A digital camera is great for this because you are able to see what you're doing and upload it to the site easily. The better your item looks on the screen, the more people will want to look at it and know more about it.

Descriptive title

When titling your listing, make sure that it catches attention. A title should be descriptive and worded so that it automatically demands the viewer's attention. Look at your item and think of the different ways you can describe it and find a catchy and unique title that will bring customers to your listing.

If it's a specific item, use the details of that item in the title. For example, you're selling a certain model of radio. Make sure that you're thoroughly describing what model it is in the title. If the buyer is not looking for that specific model, it's easy for them to pass it by without wasting time looking into the complete listing or if they are, they know that they have found what they are looking for. Using all capital letters is another good way to make your item stand out. This invokes a feeling of excitement and makes people stay on your listing longer. When reading a book, the words that stand out tend to grab your attention much more than uniform script.

Low starting bid

When scrolling through the listings on eBay, I find that if the item tends to be overpriced, I will continue to search for another that is more reasonably priced. People go on eBay to find deals. Especially if you're selling used items, you don't want to price them as if they're new. If you price your item too highly to begin with, no one will want to bid on it. Try starting your item at the price you bought it for or lower and let the bidders decide the price. If it's in enough demand, the price will raise itself without much difficulty. I know that if I see items that are initially too expensive, then I will pass them by without a second glance, so don't make that mistake when listing your items. If your item is of value, you will be getting the bids that it deserves during the bidding process.

Another factor that will turn me away from an item is the shipping costs. If a seller charges more than is necessary to ship the item, then it is a huge turn off for the buyer. Make sure that you're doing your research and placing reasonable postage on your listings. It should only cost the buyer what it would cost you to ship it.

By making your listing stand out in the auctions, you will attract viewers to look more closely at what you're selling. Once you have their attention, it is easier to have them read more about the item and ask questions about it if necessary. You want people to keep bidding on your items so that you can obtain the top selling price and gain more money from your investment. Try different methods to make your items stand out. Once your ratings start to grow, then that will become another selling point for your items. However, when you're starting out, then you will need to build your eBay business so that others will trust you.

Chapter 5- How Does eBay Work?

The concept of eBay is often misinterpreted by many people. When some look at eBay, they think of it as a place to buy cheap stuff. Others look at it as an opportunity to find unique items that not everyone has access to. Whatever the concept that a person has of eBay, one thing remains the same. People must bid for what is offered on the website.

As mentioned before, eBay is an online auction site. Businesses and individuals are able to list items on the site to either sell outright or for the public to bid on. You can either spend very little for an item or spend more reasonable prices for items than you might find in other places. eBay makes its money by charging the sellers fees for listing and selling their item on their site.

How does this affect you? Well, you can make a lot of money off of eBay in various ways. Since the fees that the site charges tend to be minimal, it makes it easier to gain a profit by selling your items with them. As you use the site more and more, there are promotions that will limit your listing fees and make it more reasonable to list your items.

Once your item is listed on the site, the general public can view your item. If they are registered with the site, they are able to bid on your item and hike the selling price up. An auction on an item typically lasts a week. At first, you might not notice that there is a lot of bidding going on with your item, but once the auction nears the end, it reaches the top of the list in its category and will gain more attention. A lot of the bidding will take place on the last day of the listing.

After selling your item, you can track when the buyer has paid, print shipping labels and communicate with the buyer. If the buyer does not pay for the item, you are able to file a dispute and get your fees refunded. After that, you are able to relist your item in another auction or offer it to the second place bidder for the price they had bidded for it.

Ebay will charge its seller's fees once a month and you pay by the method that you chose upon opening the seller account. The fees are based upon the final selling prices of the items. They tend to be very low. However, you need to take into account of these fees when you are trying to calculate your profit from your item. Another factor that you need to take into account is the shipping and handling fees. These are typically decided upon when you list your item, but you need to be aware of the prices of shipping and handling in order to price this fairly. Be careful when pricing your item for international sale because it tends to be much more expensive. I will cover more about the shipping process in a later chapter.

Understanding how the process works will help you to better navigate the site and get the most out of the experience. Getting a feel for how to sell and make sure that your online eBay business is successful will help you to sell items in the future. When you sell and raise your ratings, buyers will trust you and you're more likely to sell what you post.

Chapter 6- Amazing Your Buyer

When it comes down to it, the buyer is the most important part of the equation. The buyer is the one who choses what to buy and how much they want to pay for it. In order to run a successful eBay business, you need to take care of your buyers and impress them. How do you do that? Let's take a look at how to make your buyers keep coming back to you for future purchases.

Great communication

From the very beginning, be up front and honest about what you're selling. The worst mistake you can make is by being dishonest in how you market your item. If you what you're selling has damage or imperfections, be honest about it. A buyer who receives an item that is misrepresented is more likely to give you poor ratings, affecting your future selling abilities.

If you receive questions about your items, respond in a timely manner and be honest in your communications. The buyer is showing interest in what you're selling, give them the information that they seek. In the end, you might get a much better price for your item if you make the effort to answer all of the questions completely.

Timely shipping

Once your buyer has made payment for the item, get the item shipped as quickly as possible. I try to ship items within twenty-four hours of purchase. The buyer likes to receive what they paid good money for quickly. If the customer has special requests about how they want the item shipped, be as accommodating as possible and follow all reasonable requests. The greatest amount of feedback you will receive will be centered on the quality of the item and how quickly the item arrived.

Stand by your item

If the buyer receives the item and it's not what they had expected, stand by what you sold them. If they want a refund, give them a refund upon receiving your item back. You as a seller want to show your buyers that you're concerned with your integrity as a seller. If you get a lot of feedback about your poor items, then you are going to have trouble selling items in the future.

Your current customers will determine how you get your future customers. Seller ratings are very important to making sure you sell items in the future. People look at these ratings when they look at the item. If you have poor seller ratings, it will deter buyers from wanting to bid on your item. The fewer bids you receive, the less of a profit you will obtain for the item. You want to get the maximum value out of the items you list. That's the point on trying to sell them. Take care of your customers and they will take care of you!

Chapter 7- Shipping Your Items for Top Customer Reviews

In the previous chapters, I have talked a lot about the shipping of the item. Shipping is an important factor in selling your items on eBay because your reviews are based upon the overall customer experience. They are all tied together. Just because you sold your item doesn't mean that the sale is over. In this chapter, I'm going to give you some ideas on how to make sure that your items are properly shipped so that you have a maximum profit and a satisfied customer.

Fair shipping rates

When you list your item, the site will ask you how much you're going to charge for shipping. If you don't know, then take a look at current shipping rates for the different delivery methods. The United States Postal Service offers flat rate boxes for free. You only pay the price that is necessary upon shipping the item. If you're shipping this way, figure out what size of box will hold the item without damaging it and use that price for your shipping costs.

If you're shipping to a foreign address, then make sure that your prices for that are fair and within standard as well. I made the mistake of not putting enough of a price on shipping and I took a huge loss because the winning bidder lived overseas. Take the fact that people in other countries are very active on eBay and they buy your item, you have to ship it to them.

Proper packaging

No one wants to have their item come in the mail damaged. This can be avoided by making sure you pack and ship the item correctly. Take some time to use bubble wrap and packing peanuts to ensure that the item will arrive in the same condition you shipped it in.

Think about it this way: the mail people don't know what is in that box. It might get thrown about, crushed, and any number of mishaps can happen during the time it leaves your hands and arrives at its destination. Plan for this when you're packing it. If it's breakable or can be damaged during shipping, take the extra effort and put extra padding around it.

Putting enough postage on it

If you're shipping without a flat rate box, then it's important that there is enough postage on the package. For example, if what you're sending is in an envelope, then either have the post office clerk apply postage or make sure there is enough on the package yourself to ensure that it's delivered properly. The last thing that you want is to have it returned for improper postage and having to explain to your buyer that it will be longer than expected.

Pay for a tracking number

Customers like to be able to know where their items are in the shipping process. By providing a tracking number when you mark that the item has shipped will let them know where it is the entire time it's in between. If something should go wrong, then the customer and you can figure out where it happened and where the package is sitting.

Insure the item

If the item is breakable and holds value, it's a great idea to purchase insurance for the item in case it's lost or damaged during shipping. When using a flat rate box, insurance is included up to a certain value. If the item's selling price is above that, make a little extra effort and purchase additional insurance on it. If the item ends up lost or stolen, at least you and your buyer will be refunded the value of the item.

Take care of your buyer. When shipping your items, treat them like they are of extreme importance. You don't know what will happen between you shipping it and the buyer receiving it. It's better to plan for the worst than under plan and have something happen. The buyer ultimately makes your ratings, so be conscientious of the different factors that can take place during the entire transaction. The buyer will be grateful and so will you.

Conclusion

Thank you again for downloading this book!

I hope this book was able to help you to start a successful eBay selling venture that will help you make a ton of extra cash by finding items to resell from thrift stores. Taking the time to look through thrift stores can be a great way to make extra money. From buying the item to reselling it on eBay for a profit, you are making money from items that others want and others gave away.

The next step is to go through your local thrift store and see if you can find items that can be sold on eBay for a profit. Take the time to create a seller account on eBay and market your thrift store finds so that eBay buyers will pay top dollar for what you have found at a bargain. Be sure to take care of the buyer from the time they initially contact you until they leave their feedback for you on the website. Once you have sold a few items, you will build a reputation and be well on your way to becoming a power seller!

Finally, if you enjoyed this book, then I'd like to ask you for a favor, would you be kind enough to leave a review for this book on Amazon? It'd be greatly appreciated!

Check Out My Other Books

Below you'll find some of my other popular books that are popular on Amazon and Kindle as well. Simply click on the links below to check them out. Alternatively, you can visit my author page on Amazon to see other work done by me.

http://www.amazon.com/Unlocking-eBay-Goldmine-Maintain-Profitable-ebook/dp/B00Q7O0Z1W

http://www.amazon.com/Turning-Thrift-Store-Finds-Into-ebook/dp/B00S33XFXK

http://www.amazon.com/Unlocking-Etsy-Goldmine-Profitable-Business-ebook/dp/B00P35V5I8

http://www.amazon.com/Ultimate-Instagram-Marketing-Guide-Successful-ebook/dp/B00QUCPGWE

http://www.amazon.com/Passive-Income-Goldmine-Creative-Financial-ebook/dp/B00PGCU0LG

http://www.amazon.com/Time-Management-Strategies-Procrastination-Productivity-ebook/dp/B00SUMNIAY

Printed in Great Britain
by Amazon